GOOD DAY START WITH
GRATITUDE

THIS JOURNAL BELONGS TO :

____

TODAY'S AFFIRMATION   /   /

"

"

3 THINGS I'LL ACCOMPLISH TODAY   3 THINGS I LOOK FORWARD TO

1.   1.

2.   2.

3.   3.

TO DAY'S SCHEDULE

WHAT WOULD MAKE TO DAY GREAT?

HOW CAN I SET MYSELF FOR SUCCESS TO DAY?

HOW DO I WANT TO FEEL AT THE END OF TODAY?

GOOD DAY START WITH

GRATITUDE

TODAY'S AFFIRMATION   /   /

"

"

3 THINGS I'LL ACCOMPLISH TODAY   3 THINGS I LOOK FORWARD TO

1.   1.

2.   2.

3.   3.

TO DAY'S SCHEDULE

WHAT WOULD MAKE TO DAY GREAT?

HOW CAN I SET MYSELF FOR SUCCESS TO DAY?

HOW DO I WANT TO FEEL AT THE END OF TODAY?

SHARE YOUR JOY

GRATITUDE

TODAY'S AFFIRMATION   /   /

"

"

3 THINGS I'LL ACCOMPLISH TODAY   3 THINGS I LOOK FORWARD TO

1.   1.

2.   2.

3.   3.

TO DAY'S SCHEDULE

WHAT WOULD MAKE TO DAY GREAT?

HOW CAN I SET MYSELF FOR SUCCESS TO DAY?

HOW DO I WANT TO FEEL AT THE END OF TODAY?

TODAY'S AFFIRMATION   /   /

"

                                                                    "

3 THINGS I'LL ACCOMPLISH TODAY   3 THINGS I LOOK FORWARD TO

1.   1.

2.   2.

3.   3.

TO DAY'S SCHEDULE

WHAT WOULD MAKE TO DAY GREAT?

HOW CAN I SET MYSELF FOR SUCCESS TO DAY?

HOW DO I WANT TO FEEL AT THE END OF TODAY?

TODAY'S AFFIRMATION   /   /

"

"

3 THINGS I'LL ACCOMPLISH TODAY	3 THINGS I LOOK FORWARD TO
1.	1.
2.	2.
3.	3.

TO DAY'S SCHEDULE

WHAT WOULD MAKE TO DAY GREAT?

HOW CAN I SET MYSELF FOR SUCCESS TO DAY?

HOW DO I WANT TO FEEL AT THE END OF TODAY?

TODAY'S AFFIRMATION   /   /

"

                                                                                    "

3 THINGS I'LL ACCOMPLISH TODAY   3 THINGS I LOOK FORWARD TO

1.   1.

2.   2.

3.   3.

TO DAY'S SCHEDULE

WHAT WOULD MAKE TO DAY GREAT?

HOW CAN I SET MYSELF FOR SUCCESS TO DAY?

HOW DO I WANT TO FEEL AT THE END OF TODAY?

TODAY'S AFFIRMATION   /   /

"

"

3 THINGS I'LL ACCOMPLISH TODAY   3 THINGS I LOOK FORWARD TO

1.   1.

2.   2.

3.   3.

TO DAY'S SCHEDULE

WHAT WOULD MAKE TO DAY GREAT?

HOW CAN I SET MYSELF FOR SUCCESS TO DAY?

HOW DO I WANT TO FEEL AT THE END OF TODAY?

TODAY'S AFFIRMATION   /   /

"

"

3 THINGS I'LL ACCOMPLISH TODAY   3 THINGS I LOOK FORWARD TO

1.   1.

2.   2.

3.   3.

TO DAY'S SCHEDULE

WHAT WOULD MAKE TO DAY GREAT?

HOW CAN I SET MYSELF FOR SUCCESS TO DAY?

HOW DO I WANT TO FEEL AT THE END OF TODAY?

TODAY'S AFFIRMATION   /   /

"

"

3 THINGS I'LL ACCOMPLISH TODAY	3 THINGS I LOOK FORWARD TO
1.	1.
2.	2.
3.	3.

TO DAY'S SCHEDULE

WHAT WOULD MAKE TO DAY GREAT?

HOW CAN I SET MYSELF FOR SUCCESS TO DAY?

HOW DO I WANT TO FEEL AT THE END OF TODAY?

TODAY'S AFFIRMATION   /   /

"

"

3 THINGS I'LL ACCOMPLISH TODAY   3 THINGS I LOOK FORWARD TO

1.   1.

2.   2.

3.   3.

TO DAY'S SCHEDULE

WHAT WOULD MAKE TO DAY GREAT?

HOW CAN I SET MYSELF FOR SUCCESS TO DAY?

HOW DO I WANT TO FEEL AT THE END OF TODAY?

GRATITUDE

TODAY'S AFFIRMATION   /   /

"

                                                                              "

3 THINGS I'LL ACCOMPLISH TODAY   3 THINGS I LOOK FORWARD TO

1.   1.

2.   2.

3.   3.

TO DAY'S SCHEDULE

WHAT WOULD MAKE TO DAY GREAT?

HOW CAN I SET MYSELF FOR SUCCESS TO DAY?

HOW DO I WANT TO FEEL AT THE END OF TODAY?

TODAY'S AFFIRMATION   /   /

"

"

3 THINGS I'LL ACCOMPLISH TODAY

1.

2.

3.

3 THINGS I LOOK FORWARD TO

1.

2.

3.

TO DAY'S SCHEDULE

WHAT WOULD MAKE TO DAY GREAT?

HOW CAN I SET MYSELF FOR SUCCESS TO DAY?

HOW DO I WANT TO FEEL AT THE END OF TODAY?

TODAY'S AFFIRMATION   /   /

"

                                                                    "

3 THINGS I'LL ACCOMPLISH TODAY   3 THINGS I LOOK FORWARD TO

1.   1.

2.   2.

3.   3.

TO DAY'S SCHEDULE

WHAT WOULD MAKE TO DAY GREAT?

HOW CAN I SET MYSELF FOR SUCCESS TO DAY?

HOW DO I WANT TO FEEL AT THE END OF TODAY?

TODAY'S AFFIRMATION   /   /

"

"

3 THINGS I'LL ACCOMPLISH TODAY   3 THINGS I LOOK FORWARD TO

1.   1.

2.   2.

3.   3.

TO DAY'S SCHEDULE

WHAT WOULD MAKE TO DAY GREAT?

HOW CAN I SET MYSELF FOR SUCCESS TO DAY?

HOW DO I WANT TO FEEL AT THE END OF TODAY?

TODAY'S AFFIRMATION   /   /

"

"

3 THINGS I'LL ACCOMPLISH TODAY   3 THINGS I LOOK FORWARD TO

1.   1.

2.   2.

3.   3.

TO DAY'S SCHEDULE

WHAT WOULD MAKE TO DAY GREAT?

HOW CAN I SET MYSELF FOR SUCCESS TO DAY?

HOW DO I WANT TO FEEL AT THE END OF TODAY?

TODAY'S AFFIRMATION   /   /

"

"

3 THINGS I'LL ACCOMPLISH TODAY   3 THINGS I LOOK FORWARD TO

1.   1.

2.   2.

3.   3.

TO DAY'S SCHEDULE

WHAT WOULD MAKE TO DAY GREAT?

HOW CAN I SET MYSELF FOR SUCCESS TO DAY?

HOW DO I WANT TO FEEL AT THE END OF TODAY?

TODAY'S AFFIRMATION   /   /

"

"

3 THINGS I'LL ACCOMPLISH TODAY   3 THINGS I LOOK FORWARD TO

1.   1.

2.   2.

3.   3.

TO DAY'S SCHEDULE

WHAT WOULD MAKE TO DAY GREAT?

HOW CAN I SET MYSELF FOR SUCCESS TO DAY?

HOW DO I WANT TO FEEL AT THE END OF TODAY?

TODAY'S AFFIRMATION

/   /

"

"

3 THINGS I'LL ACCOMPLISH TODAY

1.

2.

3.

3 THINGS I LOOK FORWARD TO

1.

2.

3.

TO DAY'S SCHEDULE

WHAT WOULD MAKE TO DAY GREAT?

HOW CAN I SET MYSELF FOR SUCCESS TO DAY?

HOW DO I WANT TO FEEL AT THE END OF TODAY?

TODAY'S AFFIRMATION   /   /

"

"

3 THINGS I'LL ACCOMPLISH TODAY   3 THINGS I LOOK FORWARD TO

1.   1.

2.   2.

3.   3.

TO DAY'S SCHEDULE

WHAT WOULD MAKE TO DAY GREAT?

HOW CAN I SET MYSELF FOR SUCCESS TO DAY?

HOW DO I WANT TO FEEL AT THE END OF TODAY?

TODAY'S AFFIRMATION   /   /

"

"

3 THINGS I'LL ACCOMPLISH TODAY   3 THINGS I LOOK FORWARD TO

1.   1.

2.   2.

3.   3.

TO DAY'S SCHEDULE

WHAT WOULD MAKE TO DAY GREAT?

HOW CAN I SET MYSELF FOR SUCCESS TO DAY?

HOW DO I WANT TO FEEL AT THE END OF TODAY?

TODAY'S AFFIRMATION   /   /

"

                                                                              "

3 THINGS I'LL ACCOMPLISH TODAY   3 THINGS I LOOK FORWARD TO

1.   1.

2.   2.

3.   3.

TO DAY'S SCHEDULE

WHAT WOULD MAKE TO DAY GREAT?

HOW CAN I SET MYSELF FOR SUCCESS TO DAY?

HOW DO I WANT TO FEEL AT THE END OF TODAY?

TODAY'S AFFIRMATION   /   /

"

"

3 THINGS I'LL ACCOMPLISH TODAY   3 THINGS I LOOK FORWARD TO

1.   1.

2.   2.

3.   3.

TO DAY'S SCHEDULE

WHAT WOULD MAKE TO DAY GREAT?

HOW CAN I SET MYSELF FOR SUCCESS TO DAY?

HOW DO I WANT TO FEEL AT THE END OF TODAY?

GRATITUDE

TODAY'S AFFIRMATION   /   /

"

"

3 THINGS I'LL ACCOMPLISH TODAY   3 THINGS I LOOK FORWARD TO

1.   1.

2.   2.

3.   3.

TO DAY'S SCHEDULE

WHAT WOULD MAKE TO DAY GREAT?

HOW CAN I SET MYSELF FOR SUCCESS TO DAY?

HOW DO I WANT TO FEEL AT THE END OF TODAY?

TODAY'S AFFIRMATION   /   /

"

"

3 THINGS I'LL ACCOMPLISH TODAY   3 THINGS I LOOK FORWARD TO

1.   1.

2.   2.

3.   3.

TO DAY'S SCHEDULE

WHAT WOULD MAKE TO DAY GREAT?

HOW CAN I SET MYSELF FOR SUCCESS TO DAY?

HOW DO I WANT TO FEEL AT THE END OF TODAY?

TODAY'S AFFIRMATION   /   /

"

"

3 THINGS I'LL ACCOMPLISH TODAY   3 THINGS I LOOK FORWARD TO

1.   1.

2.   2.

3.   3.

TO DAY'S SCHEDULE

WHAT WOULD MAKE TO DAY GREAT?

HOW CAN I SET MYSELF FOR SUCCESS TO DAY?

HOW DO I WANT TO FEEL AT THE END OF TODAY?

TODAY'S AFFIRMATION   /   /

"

"

3 THINGS I'LL ACCOMPLISH TODAY   3 THINGS I LOOK FORWARD TO

1.   1.

2.   2.

3.   3.

TO DAY'S SCHEDULE

WHAT WOULD MAKE TO DAY GREAT?

HOW CAN I SET MYSELF FOR SUCCESS TO DAY?

HOW DO I WANT TO FEEL AT THE END OF TODAY?

TODAY'S AFFIRMATION   /   /

"

"

3 THINGS I'LL ACCOMPLISH TODAY   3 THINGS I LOOK FORWARD TO

1.   1.

2.   2.

3.   3.

TO DAY'S SCHEDULE

WHAT WOULD MAKE TO DAY GREAT?

HOW CAN I SET MYSELF FOR SUCCESS TO DAY?

HOW DO I WANT TO FEEL AT THE END OF TODAY?

TODAY'S AFFIRMATION

    /   /

"

"

3 THINGS I'LL ACCOMPLISH TODAY

1.

2.

3.

3 THINGS I LOOK FORWARD TO

1.

2.

3.

TO DAY'S SCHEDULE

WHAT WOULD MAKE TO DAY GREAT?

HOW CAN I SET MYSELF FOR SUCCESS TO DAY?

HOW DO I WANT TO FEEL AT THE END OF TODAY?

TODAY'S AFFIRMATION   /   /

"

"

3 THINGS I'LL ACCOMPLISH TODAY

1.

2.

3.

3 THINGS I LOOK FORWARD TO

1.

2.

3.

TO DAY'S SCHEDULE

WHAT WOULD MAKE TO DAY GREAT?

HOW CAN I SET MYSELF FOR SUCCESS TO DAY?

HOW DO I WANT TO FEEL AT THE END OF TODAY?

TODAY'S AFFIRMATION   /   /

"

"

3 THINGS I'LL ACCOMPLISH TODAY   3 THINGS I LOOK FORWARD TO

1.   1.

2.   2.

3.   3.

TO DAY'S SCHEDULE

WHAT WOULD MAKE TO DAY GREAT?

HOW CAN I SET MYSELF FOR SUCCESS TO DAY?

HOW DO I WANT TO FEEL AT THE END OF TODAY?

GRATITUDE

TODAY'S AFFIRMATION   /   /

"

"

3 THINGS I'LL ACCOMPLISH TODAY   3 THINGS I LOOK FORWARD TO

1.   1.

2.   2.

3.   3.

TO DAY'S SCHEDULE

WHAT WOULD MAKE TO DAY GREAT?

HOW CAN I SET MYSELF FOR SUCCESS TO DAY?

HOW DO I WANT TO FEEL AT THE END OF TODAY?

TODAY'S AFFIRMATION   /   /

"

"

3 THINGS I'LL ACCOMPLISH TODAY   3 THINGS I LOOK FORWARD TO

1.   1.

2.   2.

3.   3.

TO DAY'S SCHEDULE

WHAT WOULD MAKE TO DAY GREAT?

HOW CAN I SET MYSELF FOR SUCCESS TO DAY?

HOW DO I WANT TO FEEL AT THE END OF TODAY?

TODAY'S AFFIRMATION   /   /

"

"

3 THINGS I'LL ACCOMPLISH TODAY   3 THINGS I LOOK FORWARD TO

1.   1.

2.   2.

3.   3.

TO DAY'S SCHEDULE

WHAT WOULD MAKE TO DAY GREAT?

HOW CAN I SET MYSELF FOR SUCCESS TO DAY?

HOW DO I WANT TO FEEL AT THE END OF TODAY?

TODAY'S AFFIRMATION   /   /

"

"

3 THINGS I'LL ACCOMPLISH TODAY   3 THINGS I LOOK FORWARD TO

1.   1.

2.   2.

3.   3.

TO DAY'S SCHEDULE

WHAT WOULD MAKE TO DAY GREAT?

HOW CAN I SET MYSELF FOR SUCCESS TO DAY?

HOW DO I WANT TO FEEL AT THE END OF TODAY?

TODAY'S AFFIRMATION   /   /

"

"

3 THINGS I'LL ACCOMPLISH TODAY   3 THINGS I LOOK FORWARD TO

1.   1.

2.   2.

3.   3.

TODAY'S SCHEDULE

WHAT WOULD MAKE TODAY GREAT?

HOW CAN I SET MYSELF FOR SUCCESS TODAY?

HOW DO I WANT TO FEEL AT THE END OF TODAY?

TODAY'S AFFIRMATION   /   /

"

"

3 THINGS I'LL ACCOMPLISH TODAY   3 THINGS I LOOK FORWARD TO

1.   1.

2.   2.

3.   3.

TO DAY'S SCHEDULE

WHAT WOULD MAKE TO DAY GREAT?

HOW CAN I SET MYSELF FOR SUCCESS TO DAY?

HOW DO I WANT TO FEEL AT THE END OF TODAY?

TODAY'S AFFIRMATION   /   /

"

"

3 THINGS I'LL ACCOMPLISH TODAY   3 THINGS I LOOK FORWARD TO

1.   1.

2.   2.

3.   3.

TO DAY'S SCHEDULE

WHAT WOULD MAKE TO DAY GREAT?

HOW CAN I SET MYSELF FOR SUCCESS TO DAY?

HOW DO I WANT TO FEEL AT THE END OF TODAY?

TODAY'S AFFIRMATION   /   /

"

                                                    "

3 THINGS I'LL ACCOMPLISH TODAY   3 THINGS I LOOK FORWARD TO

1.   1.

2.   2.

3.   3.

TO DAY'S SCHEDULE

WHAT WOULD MAKE TO DAY GREAT?

HOW CAN I SET MYSELF FOR SUCCESS TO DAY?

HOW DO I WANT TO FEEL AT THE END OF TODAY?

TODAY'S AFFIRMATION   /   /

"

"

3 THINGS I'LL ACCOMPLISH TODAY   3 THINGS I LOOK FORWARD TO

1.   1.

2.   2.

3.   3.

TODAY'S SCHEDULE

WHAT WOULD MAKE TODAY GREAT?

HOW CAN I SET MYSELF FOR SUCCESS TODAY?

HOW DO I WANT TO FEEL AT THE END OF TODAY?

TODAY'S AFFIRMATION   /   /

"

"

3 THINGS I'LL ACCOMPLISH TODAY   3 THINGS I LOOK FORWARD TO

1.   1.

2.   2.

3.   3.

TO DAY'S SCHEDULE

WHAT WOULD MAKE TO DAY GREAT?

HOW CAN I SET MYSELF FOR SUCCESS TO DAY?

HOW DO I WANT TO FEEL AT THE END OF TODAY?

GOOD DAY START WITH

GRATITUDE

TODAY'S AFFIRMATION   /   /

"

                                                                              "

3 THINGS I'LL ACCOMPLISH TODAY	3 THINGS I LOOK FORWARD TO
1.	1.
2.	2.
3.	3.

TO DAY'S SCHEDULE

WHAT WOULD MAKE TO DAY GREAT?

HOW CAN I SET MYSELF FOR SUCCESS TO DAY?

HOW DO I WANT TO FEEL AT THE END OF TODAY?

TODAY'S AFFIRMATION   /   /

"

                                                                    "

3 THINGS I'LL ACCOMPLISH TODAY   3 THINGS I LOOK FORWARD TO

1.   1.

2.   2.

3.   3.

TO DAY'S SCHEDULE

WHAT WOULD MAKE TO DAY GREAT?

HOW CAN I SET MYSELF FOR SUCCESS TO DAY?

HOW DO I WANT TO FEEL AT THE END OF TODAY?

GOOD DAY START WITH

GRATITUDE

TODAY'S AFFIRMATION   /   /

"

"

3 THINGS I'LL ACCOMPLISH TODAY   3 THINGS I LOOK FORWARD TO

1.   1.

2.   2.

3.   3.

TO DAY'S SCHEDULE

WHAT WOULD MAKE TO DAY GREAT?

HOW CAN I SET MYSELF FOR SUCCESS TO DAY?

HOW DO I WANT TO FEEL AT THE END OF TODAY?

TODAY'S AFFIRMATION   /   /

"

"

3 THINGS I'LL ACCOMPLISH TODAY

1.

2.

3.

3 THINGS I LOOK FORWARD TO

1.

2.

3.

TO DAY'S SCHEDULE

WHAT WOULD MAKE TO DAY GREAT?

HOW CAN I SET MYSELF FOR SUCCESS TO DAY?

HOW DO I WANT TO FEEL AT THE END OF TODAY?

TODAY'S AFFIRMATION   /   /

"

"

3 THINGS I'LL ACCOMPLISH TODAY   3 THINGS I LOOK FORWARD TO

1.   1.

2.   2.

3.   3.

TO DAY'S SCHEDULE

WHAT WOULD MAKE TO DAY GREAT?

HOW CAN I SET MYSELF FOR SUCCESS TO DAY?

HOW DO I WANT TO FEEL AT THE END OF TODAY?

TODAY'S AFFIRMATION   /   /

"

"

3 THINGS I'LL ACCOMPLISH TODAY   3 THINGS I LOOK FORWARD TO

1.   1.

2.   2.

3.   3.

TO DAY'S SCHEDULE

WHAT WOULD MAKE TO DAY GREAT?

HOW CAN I SET MYSELF FOR SUCCESS TO DAY?

HOW DO I WANT TO FEEL AT THE END OF TODAY?

TODAY'S AFFIRMATION   /   /

"

                                                                    "

3 THINGS I'LL ACCOMPLISH TODAY   3 THINGS I LOOK FORWARD TO

1.   1.

2.   2.

3.   3.

TO DAY'S SCHEDULE

WHAT WOULD MAKE TO DAY GREAT?

HOW CAN I SET MYSELF FOR SUCCESS TO DAY?

HOW DO I WANT TO FEEL AT THE END OF TODAY?

TODAY'S AFFIRMATION   /   /

"

"

3 THINGS I'LL ACCOMPLISH TODAY   3 THINGS I LOOK FORWARD TO

1.   1.

2.   2.

3.   3.

TO DAY'S SCHEDULE

WHAT WOULD MAKE TO DAY GREAT?

HOW CAN I SET MYSELF FOR SUCCESS TO DAY?

HOW DO I WANT TO FEEL AT THE END OF TODAY?

GOOD DAY START WITH
GRATITUDE

TODAY'S AFFIRMATION   /   /

"

"

3 THINGS I'LL ACCOMPLISH TODAY   3 THINGS I LOOK FORWARD TO

1.   1.

2.   2.

3.   3.

TO DAY'S SCHEDULE

WHAT WOULD MAKE TO DAY GREAT?

HOW CAN I SET MYSELF FOR SUCCESS TO DAY?

HOW DO I WANT TO FEEL AT THE END OF TODAY?

TODAY'S AFFIRMATION   /   /

"

"

3 THINGS I'LL ACCOMPLISH TODAY   3 THINGS I LOOK FORWARD TO

1.   1.

2.   2.

3.   3.

TO DAY'S SCHEDULE

WHAT WOULD MAKE TO DAY GREAT?

HOW CAN I SET MYSELF FOR SUCCESS TO DAY?

HOW DO I WANT TO FEEL AT THE END OF TODAY?

TODAY'S AFFIRMATION   /   /

"

"

3 THINGS I'LL ACCOMPLISH TODAY   3 THINGS I LOOK FORWARD TO

1.   1.

2.   2.

3.   3.

TO DAY'S SCHEDULE

WHAT WOULD MAKE TO DAY GREAT?

HOW CAN I SET MYSELF FOR SUCCESS TO DAY?

HOW DO I WANT TO FEEL AT THE END OF TODAY?

TODAY'S AFFIRMATION   /   /

"

"

3 THINGS I'LL ACCOMPLISH TODAY   3 THINGS I LOOK FORWARD TO

1.   1.

2.   2.

3.   3.

TO DAY'S SCHEDULE

WHAT WOULD MAKE TO DAY GREAT?

HOW CAN I SET MYSELF FOR SUCCESS TO DAY?

HOW DO I WANT TO FEEL AT THE END OF TODAY?

TODAY'S AFFIRMATION   /   /

"

"

3 THINGS I'LL ACCOMPLISH TODAY   3 THINGS I LOOK FORWARD TO

1.   1.

2.   2.

3.   3.

TO DAY'S SCHEDULE

WHAT WOULD MAKE TO DAY GREAT?

HOW CAN I SET MYSELF FOR SUCCESS TO DAY?

HOW DO I WANT TO FEEL AT THE END OF TODAY?

TODAY'S AFFIRMATION   /   /

"

"

3 THINGS I'LL ACCOMPLISH TODAY   3 THINGS I LOOK FORWARD TO

1.   1.

2.   2.

3.   3.

TO DAY'S SCHEDULE

WHAT WOULD MAKE TO DAY GREAT?

HOW CAN I SET MYSELF FOR SUCCESS TO DAY?

HOW DO I WANT TO FEEL AT THE END OF TODAY?

TODAY'S AFFIRMATION   /   /

"

"

3 THINGS I'LL ACCOMPLISH TODAY   3 THINGS I LOOK FORWARD TO

1.   1.

2.   2.

3.   3.

TO DAY'S SCHEDULE

WHAT WOULD MAKE TO DAY GREAT?

HOW CAN I SET MYSELF FOR SUCCESS TO DAY?

HOW DO I WANT TO FEEL AT THE END OF TODAY?

TODAY'S AFFIRMATION   /   /

"

"

3 THINGS I'LL ACCOMPLISH TODAY   3 THINGS I LOOK FORWARD TO

1.   1.

2.   2.

3.   3.

TO DAY'S SCHEDULE

WHAT WOULD MAKE TO DAY GREAT?

HOW CAN I SET MYSELF FOR SUCCESS TO DAY?

HOW DO I WANT TO FEEL AT THE END OF TODAY?

GRATITUDE

TODAY'S AFFIRMATION   /   /

"

"

3 THINGS I'LL ACCOMPLISH TODAY	3 THINGS I LOOK FORWARD TO
1.	1.
2.	2.
3.	3.

TO DAY'S SCHEDULE

WHAT WOULD MAKE TO DAY GREAT?

HOW CAN I SET MYSELF FOR SUCCESS TO DAY?

HOW DO I WANT TO FEEL AT THE END OF TODAY?

TODAY'S AFFIRMATION   /   /

"

"

3 THINGS I'LL ACCOMPLISH TODAY   3 THINGS I LOOK FORWARD TO

1.   1.

2.   2.

3.   3.

TO DAY'S SCHEDULE

WHAT WOULD MAKE TO DAY GREAT?

HOW CAN I SET MYSELF FOR SUCCESS TO DAY?

HOW DO I WANT TO FEEL AT THE END OF TODAY?

GRATITUDE

TODAY'S AFFIRMATION   /   /

"

                                                                    "

3 THINGS I'LL ACCOMPLISH TODAY   3 THINGS I LOOK FORWARD TO

1.   1.

2.   2.

3.   3.

TO DAY'S SCHEDULE

WHAT WOULD MAKE TO DAY GREAT?

HOW CAN I SET MYSELF FOR SUCCESS TO DAY?

HOW DO I WANT TO FEEL AT THE END OF TODAY?

TODAY'S AFFIRMATION   /   /

"

"

3 THINGS I'LL ACCOMPLISH TODAY   3 THINGS I LOOK FORWARD TO

1.   1.

2.   2.

3.   3.

TO DAY'S SCHEDULE

WHAT WOULD MAKE TO DAY GREAT?

HOW CAN I SET MYSELF FOR SUCCESS TO DAY?

HOW DO I WANT TO FEEL AT THE END OF TODAY?

TODAY'S AFFIRMATION   /   /

"

"

3 THINGS I'LL ACCOMPLISH TODAY   3 THINGS I LOOK FORWARD TO

1.   1.

2.   2.

3.   3.

TO DAY'S SCHEDULE

WHAT WOULD MAKE TO DAY GREAT?

HOW CAN I SET MYSELF FOR SUCCESS TO DAY?

HOW DO I WANT TO FEEL AT THE END OF TODAY?

TODAY'S AFFIRMATION   /   /

"

"

3 THINGS I'LL ACCOMPLISH TODAY   3 THINGS I LOOK FORWARD TO

1.   1.

2.   2.

3.   3.

TO DAY'S SCHEDULE

WHAT WOULD MAKE TO DAY GREAT?

HOW CAN I SET MYSELF FOR SUCCESS TO DAY?

HOW DO I WANT TO FEEL AT THE END OF TODAY?

TODAY'S AFFIRMATION   /   /

"

"

3 THINGS I'LL ACCOMPLISH TODAY   3 THINGS I LOOK FORWARD TO

1.   1.

2.   2.

3.   3.

TO DAY'S SCHEDULE

WHAT WOULD MAKE TO DAY GREAT?

HOW CAN I SET MYSELF FOR SUCCESS TO DAY?

HOW DO I WANT TO FEEL AT THE END OF TODAY?

TODAY'S AFFIRMATION   /   /

"

"

3 THINGS I'LL ACCOMPLISH TODAY   3 THINGS I LOOK FORWARD TO

1.   1.

2.   2.

3.   3.

TO DAY'S SCHEDULE

WHAT WOULD MAKE TO DAY GREAT?

HOW CAN I SET MYSELF FOR SUCCESS TO DAY?

HOW DO I WANT TO FEEL AT THE END OF TODAY?

TODAY'S AFFIRMATION   /   /

"

"

3 THINGS I'LL ACCOMPLISH TODAY   3 THINGS I LOOK FORWARD TO

1.   1.

2.   2.

3.   3.

TO DAY'S SCHEDULE

WHAT WOULD MAKE TO DAY GREAT?

HOW CAN I SET MYSELF FOR SUCCESS TO DAY?

HOW DO I WANT TO FEEL AT THE END OF TODAY?

TODAY'S AFFIRMATION   /   /

"

"

3 THINGS I'LL ACCOMPLISH TODAY	3 THINGS I LOOK FORWARD TO
1.	1.
2.	2.
3.	3.

TO DAY'S SCHEDULE

WHAT WOULD MAKE TO DAY GREAT?

HOW CAN I SET MYSELF FOR SUCCESS TO DAY?

HOW DO I WANT TO FEEL AT THE END OF TODAY?

TODAY'S AFFIRMATION   /   /

"

"

3 THINGS I'LL ACCOMPLISH TODAY   3 THINGS I LOOK FORWARD TO

1.   1.

2.   2.

3.   3.

TO DAY'S SCHEDULE

WHAT WOULD MAKE TO DAY GREAT?

HOW CAN I SET MYSELF FOR SUCCESS TO DAY?

HOW DO I WANT TO FEEL AT THE END OF TODAY?

TODAY'S AFFIRMATION   /   /

"

"

3 THINGS I'LL ACCOMPLISH TODAY   3 THINGS I LOOK FORWARD TO

1.   1.

2.   2.

3.   3.

TO DAY'S SCHEDULE

WHAT WOULD MAKE TO DAY GREAT?

HOW CAN I SET MYSELF FOR SUCCESS TO DAY?

HOW DO I WANT TO FEEL AT THE END OF TODAY?

TODAY'S AFFIRMATION   /   /

"

"

3 THINGS I'LL ACCOMPLISH TODAY   3 THINGS I LOOK FORWARD TO

1.   1.

2.   2.

3.   3.

TO DAY'S SCHEDULE

WHAT WOULD MAKE TO DAY GREAT?

HOW CAN I SET MYSELF FOR SUCCESS TO DAY?

HOW DO I WANT TO FEEL AT THE END OF TODAY?

TODAY'S AFFIRMATION   /   /

"

"

3 THINGS I'LL ACCOMPLISH TODAY   3 THINGS I LOOK FORWARD TO

1.   1.

2.   2.

3.   3.

TO DAY'S SCHEDULE

WHAT WOULD MAKE TO DAY GREAT?

HOW CAN I SET MYSELF FOR SUCCESS TO DAY?

HOW DO I WANT TO FEEL AT THE END OF TODAY?

TODAY'S AFFIRMATION   /   /

"

"

3 THINGS I'LL ACCOMPLISH TODAY   3 THINGS I LOOK FORWARD TO

1.   1.

2.   2.

3.   3.

TO DAY'S SCHEDULE

WHAT WOULD MAKE TO DAY GREAT?

HOW CAN I SET MYSELF FOR SUCCESS TO DAY?

HOW DO I WANT TO FEEL AT THE END OF TODAY?

TODAY'S AFFIRMATION

"

"

3 THINGS I'LL ACCOMPLISH TODAY

1.

2.

3.

3 THINGS I LOOK FORWARD TO

1.

2.

3.

TO DAY'S SCHEDULE

WHAT WOULD MAKE TO DAY GREAT?

HOW CAN I SET MYSELF FOR SUCCESS TO DAY?

HOW DO I WANT TO FEEL AT THE END OF TODAY?

GRATITUDE

TODAY'S AFFIRMATION   /   /

"

                                                                                              "

3 THINGS I'LL ACCOMPLISH TODAY   3 THINGS I LOOK FORWARD TO

1.   1.

2.   2.

3.   3.

TO DAY'S SCHEDULE

WHAT WOULD MAKE TO DAY GREAT?

HOW CAN I SET MYSELF FOR SUCCESS TO DAY?

HOW DO I WANT TO FEEL AT THE END OF TODAY?

TODAY'S AFFIRMATION

/   /

"

"

3 THINGS I'LL ACCOMPLISH TODAY

1.

2.

3.

3 THINGS I LOOK FORWARD TO

1.

2.

3.

TO DAY'S SCHEDULE

WHAT WOULD MAKE TO DAY GREAT?

HOW CAN I SET MYSELF FOR SUCCESS TO DAY?

HOW DO I WANT TO FEEL AT THE END OF TODAY?

TODAY'S AFFIRMATION   /   /

"

"

3 THINGS I'LL ACCOMPLISH TODAY   3 THINGS I LOOK FORWARD TO

1.   1.

2.   2.

3.   3.

TO DAY'S SCHEDULE

WHAT WOULD MAKE TO DAY GREAT?

HOW CAN I SET MYSELF FOR SUCCESS TO DAY?

HOW DO I WANT TO FEEL AT THE END OF TODAY?

TODAY'S AFFIRMATION   /   /

"

"

3 THINGS I'LL ACCOMPLISH TODAY   3 THINGS I LOOK FORWARD TO

1.   1.

2.   2.

3.   3.

TO DAY'S SCHEDULE

WHAT WOULD MAKE TO DAY GREAT?

HOW CAN I SET MYSELF FOR SUCCESS TO DAY?

HOW DO I WANT TO FEEL AT THE END OF TODAY?

TODAY'S AFFIRMATION   /   /

"

"

3 THINGS I'LL ACCOMPLISH TODAY   3 THINGS I LOOK FORWARD TO

1.   1.

2.   2.

3.   3.

TO DAY'S SCHEDULE

WHAT WOULD MAKE TO DAY GREAT?

HOW CAN I SET MYSELF FOR SUCCESS TO DAY?

HOW DO I WANT TO FEEL AT THE END OF TODAY?

TODAY'S AFFIRMATION   /   /

"

                                                                    "

3 THINGS I'LL ACCOMPLISH TODAY   3 THINGS I LOOK FORWARD TO

1.   1.

2.   2.

3.   3.

TO DAY'S SCHEDULE

WHAT WOULD MAKE TO DAY GREAT?

HOW CAN I SET MYSELF FOR SUCCESS TO DAY?

HOW DO I WANT TO FEEL AT THE END OF TODAY?

TODAY'S AFFIRMATION   /   /

"

"

3 THINGS I'LL ACCOMPLISH TODAY   3 THINGS I LOOK FORWARD TO

1.   1.

2.   2.

3.   3.

TO DAY'S SCHEDULE

WHAT WOULD MAKE TO DAY GREAT?

HOW CAN I SET MYSELF FOR SUCCESS TO DAY?

HOW DO I WANT TO FEEL AT THE END OF TODAY?

TODAY'S AFFIRMATION

/   /

"

"

3 THINGS I'LL ACCOMPLISH TODAY

1.

2.

3.

3 THINGS I LOOK FORWARD TO

1.

2.

3.

TO DAY'S SCHEDULE

WHAT WOULD MAKE TO DAY GREAT?

HOW CAN I SET MYSELF FOR SUCCESS TO DAY?

HOW DO I WANT TO FEEL AT THE END OF TODAY?

TODAY'S AFFIRMATION

/   /

"

"

3 THINGS I'LL ACCOMPLISH TODAY

1.

2.

3.

3 THINGS I LOOK FORWARD TO

1.

2.

3.

TO DAY'S SCHEDULE

WHAT WOULD MAKE TO DAY GREAT?

HOW CAN I SET MYSELF FOR SUCCESS TO DAY?

HOW DO I WANT TO FEEL AT THE END OF TODAY?

TODAY'S AFFIRMATION   /   /

"

"

3 THINGS I'LL ACCOMPLISH TODAY   3 THINGS I LOOK FORWARD TO

1.   1.

2.   2.

3.   3.

TO DAY'S SCHEDULE

WHAT WOULD MAKE TO DAY GREAT?

HOW CAN I SET MYSELF FOR SUCCESS TO DAY?

HOW DO I WANT TO FEEL AT THE END OF TODAY?

TODAY'S AFFIRMATION   /   /

"

"

3 THINGS I'LL ACCOMPLISH TODAY   3 THINGS I LOOK FORWARD TO

1.   1.

2.   2.

3.   3.

TO DAY'S SCHEDULE

WHAT WOULD MAKE TO DAY GREAT?

HOW CAN I SET MYSELF FOR SUCCESS TO DAY?

HOW DO I WANT TO FEEL AT THE END OF TODAY?

TODAY'S AFFIRMATION   /   /

"

"

3 THINGS I'LL ACCOMPLISH TODAY   3 THINGS I LOOK FORWARD TO

1.   1.

2.   2.

3.   3.

TO DAY'S SCHEDULE

WHAT WOULD MAKE TO DAY GREAT?

HOW CAN I SET MYSELF FOR SUCCESS TO DAY?

HOW DO I WANT TO FEEL AT THE END OF TODAY?

GRATITUDE

TODAY'S AFFIRMATION   /   /

"

"

3 THINGS I'LL ACCOMPLISH TODAY   3 THINGS I LOOK FORWARD TO

1.   1.

2.   2.

3.   3.

TO DAY'S SCHEDULE

WHAT WOULD MAKE TO DAY GREAT?

HOW CAN I SET MYSELF FOR SUCCESS TO DAY?

HOW DO I WANT TO FEEL AT THE END OF TODAY?

TODAY'S AFFIRMATION   /   /

"

"

3 THINGS I'LL ACCOMPLISH TODAY

1.

2.

3.

3 THINGS I LOOK FORWARD TO

1.

2.

3.

TO DAY'S SCHEDULE

WHAT WOULD MAKE TO DAY GREAT?

HOW CAN I SET MYSELF FOR SUCCESS TO DAY?

HOW DO I WANT TO FEEL AT THE END OF TODAY?

TODAY'S AFFIRMATION   /   /

"

"

3 THINGS I'LL ACCOMPLISH TODAY   3 THINGS I LOOK FORWARD TO

1.   1.

2.   2.

3.   3.

TO DAY'S SCHEDULE

WHAT WOULD MAKE TO DAY GREAT?

HOW CAN I SET MYSELF FOR SUCCESS TO DAY?

HOW DO I WANT TO FEEL AT THE END OF TODAY?

TODAY'S AFFIRMATION   /   /

"

"

3 THINGS I'LL ACCOMPLISH TODAY   3 THINGS I LOOK FORWARD TO

1.   1.

2.   2.

3.   3.

TO DAY'S SCHEDULE

WHAT WOULD MAKE TO DAY GREAT?

HOW CAN I SET MYSELF FOR SUCCESS TO DAY?

HOW DO I WANT TO FEEL AT THE END OF TODAY?

TODAY'S AFFIRMATION   /   /

"

"

3 THINGS I'LL ACCOMPLISH TODAY   3 THINGS I LOOK FORWARD TO

1.   1.

2.   2.

3.   3.

TO DAY'S SCHEDULE

WHAT WOULD MAKE TO DAY GREAT?

HOW CAN I SET MYSELF FOR SUCCESS TO DAY?

HOW DO I WANT TO FEEL AT THE END OF TODAY?

TODAY'S AFFIRMATION   /   /

"

"

3 THINGS I'LL ACCOMPLISH TODAY   3 THINGS I LOOK FORWARD TO

1.   1.

2.   2.

3.   3.

TO DAY'S SCHEDULE

WHAT WOULD MAKE TO DAY GREAT?

HOW CAN I SET MYSELF FOR SUCCESS TO DAY?

HOW DO I WANT TO FEEL AT THE END OF TODAY?

TODAY'S AFFIRMATION   /   /

"

                                                                    "

3 THINGS I'LL ACCOMPLISH TODAY	3 THINGS I LOOK FORWARD TO
1.	1.
2.	2.
3.	3.

TO DAY'S SCHEDULE

WHAT WOULD MAKE TO DAY GREAT?

HOW CAN I SET MYSELF FOR SUCCESS TO DAY?

HOW DO I WANT TO FEEL AT THE END OF TODAY?

TODAY'S AFFIRMATION   /   /

"

"

3 THINGS I'LL ACCOMPLISH TODAY   3 THINGS I LOOK FORWARD TO

1.   1.

2.   2.

3.   3.

TO DAY'S SCHEDULE

WHAT WOULD MAKE TO DAY GREAT?

HOW CAN I SET MYSELF FOR SUCCESS TO DAY?

HOW DO I WANT TO FEEL AT THE END OF TODAY?

TODAY'S AFFIRMATION   /   /

"

"

3 THINGS I'LL ACCOMPLISH TODAY   3 THINGS I LOOK FORWARD TO

1.   1.

2.   2.

3.   3.

TO DAY'S SCHEDULE

WHAT WOULD MAKE TO DAY GREAT?

HOW CAN I SET MYSELF FOR SUCCESS TO DAY?

HOW DO I WANT TO FEEL AT THE END OF TODAY?

TODAY'S AFFIRMATION   /   /

        "

                                                                        "

3 THINGS I'LL ACCOMPLISH TODAY   3 THINGS I LOOK FORWARD TO

1.   1.

2.   2.

3.   3.

TO DAY'S SCHEDULE

WHAT WOULD MAKE TO DAY GREAT?

HOW CAN I SET MYSELF FOR SUCCESS TO DAY?

HOW DO I WANT TO FEEL AT THE END OF TODAY?

TODAY'S AFFIRMATION   /   /

"

"

3 THINGS I'LL ACCOMPLISH TODAY   3 THINGS I LOOK FORWARD TO

1.   1.

2.   2.

3.   3.

TO DAY'S SCHEDULE

WHAT WOULD MAKE TO DAY GREAT?

HOW CAN I SET MYSELF FOR SUCCESS TO DAY?

HOW DO I WANT TO FEEL AT THE END OF TODAY?

TODAY'S AFFIRMATION   /   /

"

"

3 THINGS I'LL ACCOMPLISH TODAY   3 THINGS I LOOK FORWARD TO

1.   1.

2.   2.

3.   3.

TO DAY'S SCHEDULE

WHAT WOULD MAKE TO DAY GREAT?

HOW CAN I SET MYSELF FOR SUCCESS TO DAY?

HOW DO I WANT TO FEEL AT THE END OF TODAY?

TODAY'S AFFIRMATION   /   /

"

                                                                              "

3 THINGS I'LL ACCOMPLISH TODAY   3 THINGS I LOOK FORWARD TO

1.   1.

2.   2.

3.   3.

TO DAY'S SCHEDULE

WHAT WOULD MAKE TO DAY GREAT?

HOW CAN I SET MYSELF FOR SUCCESS TO DAY?

HOW DO I WANT TO FEEL AT THE END OF TODAY?

TODAY'S AFFIRMATION

/   /

"

"

3 THINGS I'LL ACCOMPLISH TODAY

1.

2.

3.

3 THINGS I LOOK FORWARD TO

1.

2.

3.

TO DAY'S SCHEDULE

WHAT WOULD MAKE TO DAY GREAT?

HOW CAN I SET MYSELF FOR SUCCESS TO DAY?

HOW DO I WANT TO FEEL AT THE END OF TODAY?

TODAY'S AFFIRMATION   /   /

"

"

3 THINGS I'LL ACCOMPLISH TODAY	3 THINGS I LOOK FORWARD TO
1.	1.
2.	2.
3.	3.

TO DAY'S SCHEDULE

WHAT WOULD MAKE TO DAY GREAT?

HOW CAN I SET MYSELF FOR SUCCESS TO DAY?

HOW DO I WANT TO FEEL AT THE END OF TODAY?

TODAY'S AFFIRMATION   /   /

"

"

3 THINGS I'LL ACCOMPLISH TODAY   3 THINGS I LOOK FORWARD TO

1.   1.

2.   2.

3.   3.

TO DAY'S SCHEDULE

WHAT WOULD MAKE TO DAY GREAT?

HOW CAN I SET MYSELF FOR SUCCESS TO DAY?

HOW DO I WANT TO FEEL AT THE END OF TODAY?

TODAY'S AFFIRMATION   /   /

"

"

3 THINGS I'LL ACCOMPLISH TODAY   3 THINGS I LOOK FORWARD TO

1.   1.

2.   2.

3.   3.

TO DAY'S SCHEDULE

WHAT WOULD MAKE TO DAY GREAT?

HOW CAN I SET MYSELF FOR SUCCESS TO DAY?

HOW DO I WANT TO FEEL AT THE END OF TODAY?

TODAY'S AFFIRMATION   /   /

"

"

3 THINGS I'LL ACCOMPLISH TODAY   3 THINGS I LOOK FORWARD TO

1.   1.

2.   2.

3.   3.

TO DAY'S SCHEDULE

WHAT WOULD MAKE TO DAY GREAT?

HOW CAN I SET MYSELF FOR SUCCESS TO DAY?

HOW DO I WANT TO FEEL AT THE END OF TODAY?

TODAY'S AFFIRMATION   /   /

"

"

3 THINGS I'LL ACCOMPLISH TODAY   3 THINGS I LOOK FORWARD TO

1.   1.

2.   2.

3.   3.

TO DAY'S SCHEDULE

WHAT WOULD MAKE TO DAY GREAT?

HOW CAN I SET MYSELF FOR SUCCESS TO DAY?

HOW DO I WANT TO FEEL AT THE END OF TODAY?

TODAY'S AFFIRMATION

/   /

"

"

3 THINGS I'LL ACCOMPLISH TODAY

1.

2.

3.

3 THINGS I LOOK FORWARD TO

1.

2.

3.

TO DAY'S SCHEDULE

WHAT WOULD MAKE TO DAY GREAT?

HOW CAN I SET MYSELF FOR SUCCESS TO DAY?

HOW DO I WANT TO FEEL AT THE END OF TODAY?

TODAY'S AFFIRMATION   /   /

"

"

3 THINGS I'LL ACCOMPLISH TODAY   3 THINGS I LOOK FORWARD TO

1.   1.

2.   2.

3.   3.

TO DAY'S SCHEDULE

WHAT WOULD MAKE TO DAY GREAT?

HOW CAN I SET MYSELF FOR SUCCESS TO DAY?

HOW DO I WANT TO FEEL AT THE END OF TODAY?

TODAY'S AFFIRMATION   /   /

"

"

3 THINGS I'LL ACCOMPLISH TODAY   3 THINGS I LOOK FORWARD TO

1.   1.

2.   2.

3.   3.

TO DAY'S SCHEDULE

WHAT WOULD MAKE TO DAY GREAT?

HOW CAN I SET MYSELF FOR SUCCESS TO DAY?

HOW DO I WANT TO FEEL AT THE END OF TODAY?

TODAY'S AFFIRMATION   /   /

"

                                                                    "

3 THINGS I'LL ACCOMPLISH TODAY   3 THINGS I LOOK FORWARD TO

1.   1.

2.   2.

3.   3.

TO DAY'S SCHEDULE

WHAT WOULD MAKE TO DAY GREAT?

HOW CAN I SET MYSELF FOR SUCCESS TO DAY?

HOW DO I WANT TO FEEL AT THE END OF TODAY?

TODAY'S AFFIRMATION   /   /

"

"

3 THINGS I'LL ACCOMPLISH TODAY

1.

2.

3.

3 THINGS I LOOK FORWARD TO

1.

2.

3.

TO DAY'S SCHEDULE

WHAT WOULD MAKE TO DAY GREAT?

HOW CAN I SET MYSELF FOR SUCCESS TO DAY?

HOW DO I WANT TO FEEL AT THE END OF TODAY?

SHARE YOUR JOY

TODAY'S AFFIRMATION   /   /

"

"

3 THINGS I'LL ACCOMPLISH TODAY   3 THINGS I LOOK FORWARD TO

1.   1.

2.   2.

3.   3.

TO DAY'S SCHEDULE

WHAT WOULD MAKE TO DAY GREAT?

HOW CAN I SET MYSELF FOR SUCCESS TO DAY?

HOW DO I WANT TO FEEL AT THE END OF TODAY?

TODAY'S AFFIRMATION   /   /

"

"

3 THINGS I'LL ACCOMPLISH TODAY   3 THINGS I LOOK FORWARD TO

1.   1.

2.   2.

3.   3.

TO DAY'S SCHEDULE

WHAT WOULD MAKE TO DAY GREAT?

HOW CAN I SET MYSELF FOR SUCCESS TO DAY?

HOW DO I WANT TO FEEL AT THE END OF TODAY?

TODAY'S AFFIRMATION   /   /

"

"

3 THINGS I'LL ACCOMPLISH TODAY   3 THINGS I LOOK FORWARD TO

1.   1.

2.   2.

3.   3.

TO DAY'S SCHEDULE

WHAT WOULD MAKE TO DAY GREAT?

HOW CAN I SET MYSELF FOR SUCCESS TO DAY?

HOW DO I WANT TO FEEL AT THE END OF TODAY?

TODAY'S AFFIRMATION   /   /

"

                                                                    "

3 THINGS I'LL ACCOMPLISH TODAY   3 THINGS I LOOK FORWARD TO

1.   1.

2.   2.

3.   3.

TO DAY'S SCHEDULE

WHAT WOULD MAKE TO DAY GREAT?

HOW CAN I SET MYSELF FOR SUCCESS TO DAY?

HOW DO I WANT TO FEEL AT THE END OF TODAY?

GRATITUDE

TODAY'S AFFIRMATION   /   /

"

"

3 THINGS I'LL ACCOMPLISH TODAY	3 THINGS I LOOK FORWARD TO
1.	1.
2.	2.
3.	3.

TO DAY'S SCHEDULE

WHAT WOULD MAKE TO DAY GREAT?

HOW CAN I SET MYSELF FOR SUCCESS TO DAY?

HOW DO I WANT TO FEEL AT THE END OF TODAY?

TODAY'S AFFIRMATION   /   /

"

"

3 THINGS I'LL ACCOMPLISH TODAY

1.

2.

3.

3 THINGS I LOOK FORWARD TO

1.

2.

3.

TO DAY'S SCHEDULE

WHAT WOULD MAKE TO DAY GREAT?

HOW CAN I SET MYSELF FOR SUCCESS TO DAY?

HOW DO I WANT TO FEEL AT THE END OF TODAY?

TODAY'S AFFIRMATION   /   /

"

"

3 THINGS I'LL ACCOMPLISH TODAY   3 THINGS I LOOK FORWARD TO

1.   1.

2.   2.

3.   3.

TO DAY'S SCHEDULE

WHAT WOULD MAKE TO DAY GREAT?

HOW CAN I SET MYSELF FOR SUCCESS TO DAY?

HOW DO I WANT TO FEEL AT THE END OF TODAY?

TODAY'S AFFIRMATION   /   /

"

"

3 THINGS I'LL ACCOMPLISH TODAY   3 THINGS I LOOK FORWARD TO

1.   1.

2.   2.

3.   3.

TO DAY'S SCHEDULE

WHAT WOULD MAKE TO DAY GREAT?

HOW CAN I SET MYSELF FOR SUCCESS TO DAY?

HOW DO I WANT TO FEEL AT THE END OF TODAY?

TODAY'S AFFIRMATION   /   /

"

                                                                    "

3 THINGS I'LL ACCOMPLISH TODAY   3 THINGS I LOOK FORWARD TO

1.   1.

2.   2.

3.   3.

TO DAY'S SCHEDULE

WHAT WOULD MAKE TO DAY GREAT?

HOW CAN I SET MYSELF FOR SUCCESS TO DAY?

HOW DO I WANT TO FEEL AT THE END OF TODAY?

TODAY'S AFFIRMATION   /   /

"

"

3 THINGS I'LL ACCOMPLISH TODAY   3 THINGS I LOOK FORWARD TO

1.   1.

2.   2.

3.   3.

TO DAY'S SCHEDULE

WHAT WOULD MAKE TO DAY GREAT?

HOW CAN I SET MYSELF FOR SUCCESS TO DAY?

HOW DO I WANT TO FEEL AT THE END OF TODAY?

TODAY'S AFFIRMATION

/   /

"

"

3 THINGS I'LL ACCOMPLISH TODAY

1.

2.

3.

3 THINGS I LOOK FORWARD TO

1.

2.

3.

TO DAY'S SCHEDULE

WHAT WOULD MAKE TO DAY GREAT?

HOW CAN I SET MYSELF FOR SUCCESS TO DAY?

HOW DO I WANT TO FEEL AT THE END OF TODAY?

TODAY'S AFFIRMATION   /   /

"

"

3 THINGS I'LL ACCOMPLISH TODAY   3 THINGS I LOOK FORWARD TO

1.   1.

2.   2.

3.   3.

TO DAY'S SCHEDULE

WHAT WOULD MAKE TO DAY GREAT?

HOW CAN I SET MYSELF FOR SUCCESS TO DAY?

HOW DO I WANT TO FEEL AT THE END OF TODAY?

TODAY'S AFFIRMATION

/   /

"

"

3 THINGS I'LL ACCOMPLISH TODAY

1.

2.

3.

3 THINGS I LOOK FORWARD TO

1.

2.

3.

TO DAY'S SCHEDULE

WHAT WOULD MAKE TO DAY GREAT?

HOW CAN I SET MYSELF FOR SUCCESS TO DAY?

HOW DO I WANT TO FEEL AT THE END OF TODAY?

TODAY'S AFFIRMATION   /   /

“

”

3 THINGS I'LL ACCOMPLISH TODAY   3 THINGS I LOOK FORWARD TO

1.   1.

2.   2.

3.   3.

TO DAY'S SCHEDULE

WHAT WOULD MAKE TO DAY GREAT?

HOW CAN I SET MYSELF FOR SUCCESS TO DAY?

HOW DO I WANT TO FEEL AT THE END OF TODAY?

TODAY'S AFFIRMATION   /   /

"

"

3 THINGS I'LL ACCOMPLISH TODAY   3 THINGS I LOOK FORWARD TO

1.   1.

2.   2.

3.   3.

TO DAY'S SCHEDULE

WHAT WOULD MAKE TO DAY GREAT?

HOW CAN I SET MYSELF FOR SUCCESS TO DAY?

HOW DO I WANT TO FEEL AT THE END OF TODAY?

TODAY'S AFFIRMATION   /   /

"

"

3 THINGS I'LL ACCOMPLISH TODAY   3 THINGS I LOOK FORWARD TO

1.   1.

2.   2.

3.   3.

TO DAY'S SCHEDULE

WHAT WOULD MAKE TO DAY GREAT?

HOW CAN I SET MYSELF FOR SUCCESS TO DAY?

HOW DO I WANT TO FEEL AT THE END OF TODAY?

TODAY'S AFFIRMATION   /   /

"

"

3 THINGS I'LL ACCOMPLISH TODAY   3 THINGS I LOOK FORWARD TO

1.   1.

2.   2.

3.   3.

TO DAY'S SCHEDULE

WHAT WOULD MAKE TO DAY GREAT?

HOW CAN I SET MYSELF FOR SUCCESS TO DAY?

HOW DO I WANT TO FEEL AT THE END OF TODAY?

GRATITUDE

TODAY'S AFFIRMATION   /   /

"

"

3 THINGS I'LL ACCOMPLISH TODAY

1.

2.

3.

3 THINGS I LOOK FORWARD TO

1.

2.

3.

TO DAY'S SCHEDULE

WHAT WOULD MAKE TO DAY GREAT?

HOW CAN I SET MYSELF FOR SUCCESS TO DAY?

HOW DO I WANT TO FEEL AT THE END OF TODAY?

TODAY'S AFFIRMATION   /   /

"

                                                                    "

3 THINGS I'LL ACCOMPLISH TODAY   3 THINGS I LOOK FORWARD TO

1.   1.

2.   2.

3.   3.

TO DAY'S SCHEDULE

WHAT WOULD MAKE TO DAY GREAT?

HOW CAN I SET MYSELF FOR SUCCESS TO DAY?

HOW DO I WANT TO FEEL AT THE END OF TODAY?

TODAY'S AFFIRMATION   /   /

"

"

3 THINGS I'LL ACCOMPLISH TODAY   3 THINGS I LOOK FORWARD TO

1.   1.

2.   2.

3.   3.

TO DAY'S SCHEDULE

WHAT WOULD MAKE TO DAY GREAT?

HOW CAN I SET MYSELF FOR SUCCESS TO DAY?

HOW DO I WANT TO FEEL AT THE END OF TODAY?

TODAY'S AFFIRMATION   /   /

"

"

3 THINGS I'LL ACCOMPLISH TODAY	3 THINGS I LOOK FORWARD TO
1.	1.
2.	2.
3.	3.

TO DAY'S SCHEDULE

WHAT WOULD MAKE TO DAY GREAT?

HOW CAN I SET MYSELF FOR SUCCESS TO DAY?

HOW DO I WANT TO FEEL AT THE END OF TODAY?

TODAY'S AFFIRMATION   /   /

"

"

3 THINGS I'LL ACCOMPLISH TODAY	3 THINGS I LOOK FORWARD TO
1.	1.
2.	2.
3.	3.

TO DAY'S SCHEDULE

WHAT WOULD MAKE TO DAY GREAT?

HOW CAN I SET MYSELF FOR SUCCESS TO DAY?

HOW DO I WANT TO FEEL AT THE END OF TODAY?

TODAY'S AFFIRMATION   /   /

"

                                                            "

3 THINGS I'LL ACCOMPLISH TODAY   3 THINGS I LOOK FORWARD TO

1.   1.

2.   2.

3.   3.

TO DAY'S SCHEDULE

WHAT WOULD MAKE TO DAY GREAT?

HOW CAN I SET MYSELF FOR SUCCESS TO DAY?

HOW DO I WANT TO FEEL AT THE END OF TODAY?

TODAY'S AFFIRMATION   /   /

"

"

3 THINGS I'LL ACCOMPLISH TODAY   3 THINGS I LOOK FORWARD TO

1.   1.

2.   2.

3.   3.

TO DAY'S SCHEDULE

WHAT WOULD MAKE TO DAY GREAT?

HOW CAN I SET MYSELF FOR SUCCESS TO DAY?

HOW DO I WANT TO FEEL AT THE END OF TODAY?

TODAY'S AFFIRMATION   /   /

"

                                                    "

3 THINGS I'LL ACCOMPLISH TODAY   3 THINGS I LOOK FORWARD TO

1.   1.

2.   2.

3.   3.

TO DAY'S SCHEDULE

WHAT WOULD MAKE TO DAY GREAT?

HOW CAN I SET MYSELF FOR SUCCESS TO DAY?

HOW DO I WANT TO FEEL AT THE END OF TODAY?

TODAY'S AFFIRMATION   /   /

"

"

3 THINGS I'LL ACCOMPLISH TODAY   3 THINGS I LOOK FORWARD TO

1.   1.

2.   2.

3.   3.

TO DAY'S SCHEDULE

WHAT WOULD MAKE TO DAY GREAT?

HOW CAN I SET MYSELF FOR SUCCESS TO DAY?

HOW DO I WANT TO FEEL AT THE END OF TODAY?

GRATITUDE

TODAY'S AFFIRMATION   /   /

"

"

3 THINGS I'LL ACCOMPLISH TODAY   3 THINGS I LOOK FORWARD TO

1.   1.

2.   2.

3.   3.

TO DAY'S SCHEDULE

WHAT WOULD MAKE TO DAY GREAT?

HOW CAN I SET MYSELF FOR SUCCESS TO DAY?

HOW DO I WANT TO FEEL AT THE END OF TODAY?

TODAY'S AFFIRMATION   /   /

"

"

3 THINGS I'LL ACCOMPLISH TODAY   3 THINGS I LOOK FORWARD TO

1.   1.

2.   2.

3.   3.

TO DAY'S SCHEDULE

WHAT WOULD MAKE TO DAY GREAT?

HOW CAN I SET MYSELF FOR SUCCESS TO DAY?

HOW DO I WANT TO FEEL AT THE END OF TODAY?

TODAY'S AFFIRMATION   /   /

"

                                                                        "

3 THINGS I'LL ACCOMPLISH TODAY   3 THINGS I LOOK FORWARD TO

1.   1.

2.   2.

3.   3.

TO DAY'S SCHEDULE

WHAT WOULD MAKE TO DAY GREAT?

HOW CAN I SET MYSELF FOR SUCCESS TO DAY?

HOW DO I WANT TO FEEL AT THE END OF TODAY?

TODAY'S AFFIRMATION   /   /

"

"

3 THINGS I'LL ACCOMPLISH TODAY   3 THINGS I LOOK FORWARD TO

1.   1.

2.   2.

3.   3.

TO DAY'S SCHEDULE

WHAT WOULD MAKE TO DAY GREAT?

HOW CAN I SET MYSELF FOR SUCCESS TO DAY?

HOW DO I WANT TO FEEL AT THE END OF TODAY?

TODAY'S AFFIRMATION   /   /

"

                                                                    "

3 THINGS I'LL ACCOMPLISH TODAY   3 THINGS I LOOK FORWARD TO

1.   1.

2.   2.

3.   3.

TO DAY'S SCHEDULE

WHAT WOULD MAKE TO DAY GREAT?

HOW CAN I SET MYSELF FOR SUCCESS TO DAY?

HOW DO I WANT TO FEEL AT THE END OF TODAY?

TODAY'S AFFIRMATION   /   /

"

"

3 THINGS I'LL ACCOMPLISH TODAY   3 THINGS I LOOK FORWARD TO

1.   1.

2.   2.

3.   3.

TO DAY'S SCHEDULE

WHAT WOULD MAKE TO DAY GREAT?

HOW CAN I SET MYSELF FOR SUCCESS TO DAY?

HOW DO I WANT TO FEEL AT THE END OF TODAY?

TODAY'S AFFIRMATION   /   /

"

                                                                                          "

3 THINGS I'LL ACCOMPLISH TODAY   3 THINGS I LOOK FORWARD TO

1.   1.

2.   2.

3.   3.

TO DAY'S SCHEDULE

WHAT WOULD MAKE TO DAY GREAT?

HOW CAN I SET MYSELF FOR SUCCESS TO DAY?

HOW DO I WANT TO FEEL AT THE END OF TODAY?

TODAY'S AFFIRMATION   /   /

"

"

3 THINGS I'LL ACCOMPLISH TODAY   3 THINGS I LOOK FORWARD TO

1.   1.

2.   2.

3.   3.

TO DAY'S SCHEDULE

WHAT WOULD MAKE TO DAY GREAT?

HOW CAN I SET MYSELF FOR SUCCESS TO DAY?

HOW DO I WANT TO FEEL AT THE END OF TODAY?

TODAY'S AFFIRMATION   /   /

"

"

3 THINGS I'LL ACCOMPLISH TODAY   3 THINGS I LOOK FORWARD TO

1.   1.

2.   2.

3.   3.

TO DAY'S SCHEDULE

WHAT WOULD MAKE TO DAY GREAT?

HOW CAN I SET MYSELF FOR SUCCESS TO DAY?

HOW DO I WANT TO FEEL AT THE END OF TODAY?

TODAY'S AFFIRMATION

/   /

"

"

3 THINGS I'LL ACCOMPLISH TODAY

1.

2.

3.

3 THINGS I LOOK FORWARD TO

1.

2.

3.

TO DAY'S SCHEDULE

WHAT WOULD MAKE TO DAY GREAT?

HOW CAN I SET MYSELF FOR SUCCESS TO DAY?

HOW DO I WANT TO FEEL AT THE END OF TODAY?

TODAY'S AFFIRMATION   /   /

"

"

3 THINGS I'LL ACCOMPLISH TODAY   3 THINGS I LOOK FORWARD TO

1.   1.

2.   2.

3.   3.

TO DAY'S SCHEDULE

WHAT WOULD MAKE TO DAY GREAT?

HOW CAN I SET MYSELF FOR SUCCESS TO DAY?

HOW DO I WANT TO FEEL AT THE END OF TODAY?

GRATITUDE

TODAY'S AFFIRMATION   /   /

"

"

3 THINGS I'LL ACCOMPLISH TODAY   3 THINGS I LOOK FORWARD TO

1.   1.

2.   2.

3.   3.

TO DAY'S SCHEDULE

WHAT WOULD MAKE TO DAY GREAT?

HOW CAN I SET MYSELF FOR SUCCESS TO DAY?

HOW DO I WANT TO FEEL AT THE END OF TODAY?

TODAY'S AFFIRMATION   /   /

"

"

3 THINGS I'LL ACCOMPLISH TODAY   3 THINGS I LOOK FORWARD TO

1.   1.

2.   2.

3.   3.

TO DAY'S SCHEDULE

WHAT WOULD MAKE TO DAY GREAT?

HOW CAN I SET MYSELF FOR SUCCESS TO DAY?

HOW DO I WANT TO FEEL AT THE END OF TODAY?

TODAY'S AFFIRMATION   /   /

"

"

3 THINGS I'LL ACCOMPLISH TODAY   3 THINGS I LOOK FORWARD TO

1.   1.

2.   2.

3.   3.

TO DAY'S SCHEDULE

WHAT WOULD MAKE TO DAY GREAT?

HOW CAN I SET MYSELF FOR SUCCESS TO DAY?

HOW DO I WANT TO FEEL AT THE END OF TODAY?

GOOD DAY START WITH
GRATITUDE

TODAY'S AFFIRMATION   /   /

"

"

3 THINGS I'LL ACCOMPLISH TODAY	3 THINGS I LOOK FORWARD TO
1.	1.
2.	2.
3.	3.

TO DAY'S SCHEDULE

WHAT WOULD MAKE TO DAY GREAT?

HOW CAN I SET MYSELF FOR SUCCESS TO DAY?

HOW DO I WANT TO FEEL AT THE END OF TODAY?

TODAY'S AFFIRMATION

/   /

"

"

3 THINGS I'LL ACCOMPLISH TODAY

1.

2.

3.

3 THINGS I LOOK FORWARD TO

1.

2.

3.

TO DAY'S SCHEDULE

WHAT WOULD MAKE TO DAY GREAT?

HOW CAN I SET MYSELF FOR SUCCESS TO DAY?

HOW DO I WANT TO FEEL AT THE END OF TODAY?

TODAY'S AFFIRMATION   /   /

"

                                                                    "

3 THINGS I'LL ACCOMPLISH TODAY   3 THINGS I LOOK FORWARD TO

1.   1.

2.   2.

3.   3.

TO DAY'S SCHEDULE

WHAT WOULD MAKE TO DAY GREAT?

HOW CAN I SET MYSELF FOR SUCCESS TO DAY?

HOW DO I WANT TO FEEL AT THE END OF TODAY?

TODAY'S AFFIRMATION   /   /

"

"

3 THINGS I'LL ACCOMPLISH TODAY   3 THINGS I LOOK FORWARD TO

1.   1.

2.   2.

3.   3.

TO DAY'S SCHEDULE

WHAT WOULD MAKE TO DAY GREAT?

HOW CAN I SET MYSELF FOR SUCCESS TO DAY?

HOW DO I WANT TO FEEL AT THE END OF TODAY?

GOOD DAY START WITH

GRATITUDE

TODAY'S AFFIRMATION   /   /

"

"

3 THINGS I'LL ACCOMPLISH TODAY	3 THINGS I LOOK FORWARD TO
1.	1.
2.	2.
3.	3.

TO DAY'S SCHEDULE

WHAT WOULD MAKE TO DAY GREAT?

HOW CAN I SET MYSELF FOR SUCCESS TO DAY?

HOW DO I WANT TO FEEL AT THE END OF TODAY?

TODAY'S AFFIRMATION   /   /

"

                                                                    "

3 THINGS I'LL ACCOMPLISH TODAY   3 THINGS I LOOK FORWARD TO

1.   1.

2.   2.

3.   3.

TO DAY'S SCHEDULE

WHAT WOULD MAKE TO DAY GREAT?

HOW CAN I SET MYSELF FOR SUCCESS TO DAY?

HOW DO I WANT TO FEEL AT THE END OF TODAY?

TODAY'S AFFIRMATION   /   /

"

                                                              "

3 THINGS I'LL ACCOMPLISH TODAY   3 THINGS I LOOK FORWARD TO

1.   1.

2.   2.

3.   3.

TO DAY'S SCHEDULE

WHAT WOULD MAKE TO DAY GREAT?

HOW CAN I SET MYSELF FOR SUCCESS TO DAY?

HOW DO I WANT TO FEEL AT THE END OF TODAY?

TODAY'S AFFIRMATION   /   /

"

"

3 THINGS I'LL ACCOMPLISH TODAY	3 THINGS I LOOK FORWARD TO
1.	1.
2.	2.
3.	3.

TO DAY'S SCHEDULE

WHAT WOULD MAKE TO DAY GREAT?

HOW CAN I SET MYSELF FOR SUCCESS TO DAY?

HOW DO I WANT TO FEEL AT THE END OF TODAY?

TODAY'S AFFIRMATION   /   /

"

                                                                    "

3 THINGS I'LL ACCOMPLISH TODAY   3 THINGS I LOOK FORWARD TO

1.   1.

2.   2.

3.   3.

TO DAY'S SCHEDULE

WHAT WOULD MAKE TO DAY GREAT?

HOW CAN I SET MYSELF FOR SUCCESS TO DAY?

HOW DO I WANT TO FEEL AT THE END OF TODAY?

TODAY'S AFFIRMATION   /   /

"

"

3 THINGS I'LL ACCOMPLISH TODAY   3 THINGS I LOOK FORWARD TO

1.   1.

2.   2.

3.   3.

TO DAY'S SCHEDULE

WHAT WOULD MAKE TO DAY GREAT?

HOW CAN I SET MYSELF FOR SUCCESS TO DAY?

HOW DO I WANT TO FEEL AT THE END OF TODAY?

TODAY'S AFFIRMATION   /   /

"

"

3 THINGS I'LL ACCOMPLISH TODAY   3 THINGS I LOOK FORWARD TO

1.   1.

2.   2.

3.   3.

TO DAY'S SCHEDULE

WHAT WOULD MAKE TO DAY GREAT?

HOW CAN I SET MYSELF FOR SUCCESS TO DAY?

HOW DO I WANT TO FEEL AT THE END OF TODAY?

TODAY'S AFFIRMATION   /   /

"

"

3 THINGS I'LL ACCOMPLISH TODAY   3 THINGS I LOOK FORWARD TO

1.   1.

2.   2.

3.   3.

TO DAY'S SCHEDULE

WHAT WOULD MAKE TO DAY GREAT?

HOW CAN I SET MYSELF FOR SUCCESS TO DAY?

HOW DO I WANT TO FEEL AT THE END OF TODAY?

TODAY'S AFFIRMATION   /   /

"

"

3 THINGS I'LL ACCOMPLISH TODAY   3 THINGS I LOOK FORWARD TO

1.   1.

2.   2.

3.   3.

TO DAY'S SCHEDULE

WHAT WOULD MAKE TO DAY GREAT?

HOW CAN I SET MYSELF FOR SUCCESS TO DAY?

HOW DO I WANT TO FEEL AT THE END OF TODAY?

TODAY'S AFFIRMATION   /   /

"

"

3 THINGS I'LL ACCOMPLISH TODAY   3 THINGS I LOOK FORWARD TO

1.   1.

2.   2.

3.   3.

TO DAY'S SCHEDULE

WHAT WOULD MAKE TO DAY GREAT?

HOW CAN I SET MYSELF FOR SUCCESS TO DAY?

HOW DO I WANT TO FEEL AT THE END OF TODAY?

TODAY'S AFFIRMATION   /   /

          "

                                                                         "

3 THINGS I'LL ACCOMPLISH TODAY   3 THINGS I LOOK FORWARD TO

1.   1.

2.   2.

3.   3.

TO DAY'S SCHEDULE

WHAT WOULD MAKE TO DAY GREAT?

HOW CAN I SET MYSELF FOR SUCCESS TO DAY?

HOW DO I WANT TO FEEL AT THE END OF TODAY?

TODAY'S AFFIRMATION   /   /

"

"

3 THINGS I'LL ACCOMPLISH TODAY   3 THINGS I LOOK FORWARD TO

1.   1.

2.   2.

3.   3.

TO DAY'S SCHEDULE

WHAT WOULD MAKE TO DAY GREAT?

HOW CAN I SET MYSELF FOR SUCCESS TO DAY?

HOW DO I WANT TO FEEL AT THE END OF TODAY?

GOOD DAY START WITH
GRATITUDE

TODAY'S AFFIRMATION   /   /

"

                                                            "

3 THINGS I'LL ACCOMPLISH TODAY   3 THINGS I LOOK FORWARD TO

1.   1.

2.   2.

3.   3.

TO DAY'S SCHEDULE

WHAT WOULD MAKE TO DAY GREAT?

HOW CAN I SET MYSELF FOR SUCCESS TO DAY?

HOW DO I WANT TO FEEL AT THE END OF TODAY?

TODAY'S AFFIRMATION   /   /

"

"

3 THINGS I'LL ACCOMPLISH TODAY   3 THINGS I LOOK FORWARD TO

1.   1.

2.   2.

3.   3.

TO DAY'S SCHEDULE

WHAT WOULD MAKE TO DAY GREAT?

HOW CAN I SET MYSELF FOR SUCCESS TO DAY?

HOW DO I WANT TO FEEL AT THE END OF TODAY?

GOOD DAY START WITH
GRATITUDE

TODAY'S AFFIRMATION   /   /

"

                                                                              "

3 THINGS I'LL ACCOMPLISH TODAY   3 THINGS I LOOK FORWARD TO

1.   1.

2.   2.

3.   3.

TO DAY'S SCHEDULE

WHAT WOULD MAKE TO DAY GREAT?

HOW CAN I SET MYSELF FOR SUCCESS TO DAY?

HOW DO I WANT TO FEEL AT THE END OF TODAY?

TODAY'S AFFIRMATION   /   /

"

"

3 THINGS I'LL ACCOMPLISH TODAY   3 THINGS I LOOK FORWARD TO

1.   1.

2.   2.

3.   3.

TO DAY'S SCHEDULE

WHAT WOULD MAKE TO DAY GREAT?

HOW CAN I SET MYSELF FOR SUCCESS TO DAY?

HOW DO I WANT TO FEEL AT THE END OF TODAY?

TODAY'S AFFIRMATION   /   /

"

"

3 THINGS I'LL ACCOMPLISH TODAY   3 THINGS I LOOK FORWARD TO

1.   1.

2.   2.

3.   3.

TO DAY'S SCHEDULE

WHAT WOULD MAKE TO DAY GREAT?

HOW CAN I SET MYSELF FOR SUCCESS TO DAY?

HOW DO I WANT TO FEEL AT THE END OF TODAY?

TODAY'S AFFIRMATION   /   /

"

"

3 THINGS I'LL ACCOMPLISH TODAY   3 THINGS I LOOK FORWARD TO

1.   1.

2.   2.

3.   3.

TO DAY'S SCHEDULE

WHAT WOULD MAKE TO DAY GREAT?

HOW CAN I SET MYSELF FOR SUCCESS TO DAY?

HOW DO I WANT TO FEEL AT THE END OF TODAY?

GOOD DAY START WITH
GRATITUDE

TODAY'S AFFIRMATION   /   /

"

                                                                    "

3 THINGS I'LL ACCOMPLISH TODAY   3 THINGS I LOOK FORWARD TO

1.   1.

2.   2.

3.   3.

TO DAY'S SCHEDULE

WHAT WOULD MAKE TO DAY GREAT?

HOW CAN I SET MYSELF FOR SUCCESS TO DAY?

HOW DO I WANT TO FEEL AT THE END OF TODAY?

TODAY'S AFFIRMATION   /   /

"

                                                                              "

3 THINGS I'LL ACCOMPLISH TODAY   3 THINGS I LOOK FORWARD TO

1.   1.

2.   2.

3.   3.

TO DAY'S SCHEDULE

WHAT WOULD MAKE TO DAY GREAT?

HOW CAN I SET MYSELF FOR SUCCESS TO DAY?

HOW DO I WANT TO FEEL AT THE END OF TODAY?

TODAY'S AFFIRMATION   /   /

"

"

3 THINGS I'LL ACCOMPLISH TODAY   3 THINGS I LOOK FORWARD TO

1.   1.

2.   2.

3.   3.

TO DAY'S SCHEDULE

WHAT WOULD MAKE TO DAY GREAT?

HOW CAN I SET MYSELF FOR SUCCESS TO DAY?

HOW DO I WANT TO FEEL AT THE END OF TODAY?

GOOD DAY START WITH

GRATITUDE

TODAY'S AFFIRMATION   /   /

"

                                                                          "

3 THINGS I'LL ACCOMPLISH TODAY	3 THINGS I LOOK FORWARD TO
1.	1.
2.	2.
3.	3.

TO DAY'S SCHEDULE

WHAT WOULD MAKE TO DAY GREAT?

HOW CAN I SET MYSELF FOR SUCCESS TO DAY?

HOW DO I WANT TO FEEL AT THE END OF TODAY?

GOOD DAY START WITH
GRATITUDE

TODAY'S AFFIRMATION   /   /

"

                                                                    "

3 THINGS I'LL ACCOMPLISH TODAY   3 THINGS I LOOK FORWARD TO

1.   1.

2.   2.

3.   3.

TO DAY'S SCHEDULE

WHAT WOULD MAKE TO DAY GREAT?

HOW CAN I SET MYSELF FOR SUCCESS TO DAY?

HOW DO I WANT TO FEEL AT THE END OF TODAY?

TODAY'S AFFIRMATION

/   /

"

"

3 THINGS I'LL ACCOMPLISH TODAY

1.

2.

3.

3 THINGS I LOOK FORWARD TO

1.

2.

3.

TO DAY'S SCHEDULE

WHAT WOULD MAKE TO DAY GREAT?

HOW CAN I SET MYSELF FOR SUCCESS TO DAY?

HOW DO I WANT TO FEEL AT THE END OF TODAY?

TODAY'S AFFIRMATION   /   /

"

"

3 THINGS I'LL ACCOMPLISH TODAY   3 THINGS I LOOK FORWARD TO

1.   1.

2.   2.

3.   3.

TO DAY'S SCHEDULE

WHAT WOULD MAKE TO DAY GREAT?

HOW CAN I SET MYSELF FOR SUCCESS TO DAY?

HOW DO I WANT TO FEEL AT THE END OF TODAY?

TODAY'S AFFIRMATION   /   /

"

                                                                      "

3 THINGS I'LL ACCOMPLISH TODAY   3 THINGS I LOOK FORWARD TO

1.   1.

2.   2.

3.   3.

TO DAY'S SCHEDULE

WHAT WOULD MAKE TO DAY GREAT?

HOW CAN I SET MYSELF FOR SUCCESS TO DAY?

HOW DO I WANT TO FEEL AT THE END OF TODAY?

TODAY'S AFFIRMATION   /   /

    "

                                                                              "

3 THINGS I'LL ACCOMPLISH TODAY   3 THINGS I LOOK FORWARD TO

1.   1.

2.   2.

3.   3.

TO DAY'S SCHEDULE

WHAT WOULD MAKE TO DAY GREAT?

HOW CAN I SET MYSELF FOR SUCCESS TO DAY?

HOW DO I WANT TO FEEL AT THE END OF TODAY?

TODAY'S AFFIRMATION   /   /

"

                                                                            "

3 THINGS I'LL ACCOMPLISH TODAY   3 THINGS I LOOK FORWARD TO

1.   1.

2.   2.

3.   3.

TO DAY'S SCHEDULE

WHAT WOULD MAKE TO DAY GREAT?

HOW CAN I SET MYSELF FOR SUCCESS TO DAY?

HOW DO I WANT TO FEEL AT THE END OF TODAY?

TODAY'S AFFIRMATION   /   /

"

                                                                          "

3 THINGS I'LL ACCOMPLISH TODAY   3 THINGS I LOOK FORWARD TO

1.   1.

2.   2.

3.   3.

TO DAY'S SCHEDULE

WHAT WOULD MAKE TO DAY GREAT?

HOW CAN I SET MYSELF FOR SUCCESS TO DAY?

HOW DO I WANT TO FEEL AT THE END OF TODAY?

TODAY'S AFFIRMATION   /   /

"

"

3 THINGS I'LL ACCOMPLISH TODAY   3 THINGS I LOOK FORWARD TO

1.   1.

2.   2.

3.   3.

TO DAY'S SCHEDULE

WHAT WOULD MAKE TO DAY GREAT?

HOW CAN I SET MYSELF FOR SUCCESS TO DAY?

HOW DO I WANT TO FEEL AT THE END OF TODAY?

GOOD DAY START WITH

GRATITUDE

TODAY'S AFFIRMATION   /   /

"

"

3 THINGS I'LL ACCOMPLISH TODAY	3 THINGS I LOOK FORWARD TO
1.	1.
2.	2.
3.	3.

TO DAY'S SCHEDULE

WHAT WOULD MAKE TO DAY GREAT?

HOW CAN I SET MYSELF FOR SUCCESS TO DAY?

HOW DO I WANT TO FEEL AT THE END OF TODAY?